D1614314

Endangered RAIN FOREST ANIMALS

SAVE EARTH'S ANIMALS!

Marie Allgor

PowerKiDS press.

New York

Published in 2013 by The Rosen Publishing Group, Inc.
29 East 21st Street, New York, NY 10010

First Edition

Editor: Jennifer Way
Book Design: Julio Gil

Photo Credits: Cover John Kaprielian/Photo Researchers/Getty Images; pp. 4, 11 RFCD GeoAtlas; p. 5 Nacivet/Photographer's Choice/Getty Images; p. 5 (inset) KKulikov/Shutterstock.com; pp. 6–7 Uryadnikov Sergey/Shutterstock.com; p. 8 Peter Wollinga/Shutterstock.com; p. 9 Alexander Chaikin/Shutterstock.com; pp. 10, 11, 22 iStockphoto/Thinkstock; p. 12 Dmitry Rukhlenko/Shutterstock.com; p. 13 (main) indiangypsy/Shutterstock.com; p. 13 (inset) Tom Brakefield/Stockbyte/Thinkstock; p. 14 holbox/Shutterstock.com; p. 15 worldswildlifewonders/Shutterstock.com; p. 16 Jen St. Louis Photography/Getty Images; p. 17 Danita Delimont/Gallo Images/Getty Images; p. 18 Anan Kaewkhammul/Shutterstock.com; p. 19 Steve Cooper/Photo Researchers/Getty Images; p. 20 Zaggy/Shutterstock.com; p. 21 Frans Lemmens/Iconica/Getty Images; p. 22 iStockphoto/Thinkstock.

Library of Congress Cataloging-in-Publication Data

Allgor, Marie.
Endangered rain forest animals / By Marie Allgor. — 1st ed.
    p. cm. — (Save earth's animals!)
Includes index.
ISBN 978-1-4488-7422-4 (library binding) — ISBN 978-1-4488-7495-8 (pbk.) —
ISBN 978-1-4488-7569-6 (6-pack)
1. Endangered species—Tropics–Juvenile literature. 2. Rain forest animals—Juvenile literature. 3. Rain forest ecology—Juvenile literature. 4. Wildlife conservation—Juvenile literature. I. Title.
QL83.A44 2013
578.68—dc23
                                        2011050665

Manufactured in China

CPSIA Compliance Information: Batch # WKTS12PK: For Further Information contact Rosen Publishing, New York, New York at 1-800-237-9932

Contents

Welcome to the Rain Forest!

Rain forests are places with lots of rainfall and tall trees. More than half of the world's plants and animals live in these forests. This fact might make you think that animals in the rain forest are doing fine. This is not true, though. Huge areas of rain

This map shows where rain forest biomes are found.

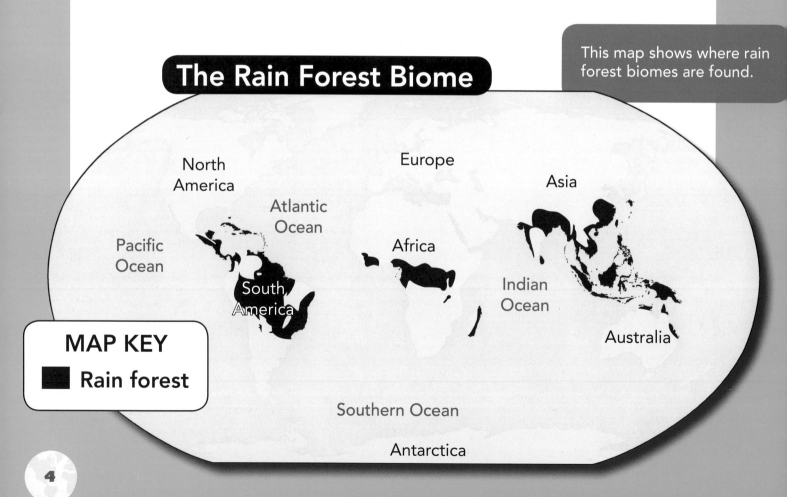

The Rain Forest Biome

North America

Europe

Asia

Atlantic Ocean

Pacific Ocean

Africa

South America

Indian Ocean

Australia

MAP KEY

█ Rain forest

Southern Ocean

Antarctica

About 6 percent of Earth is covered in rain forests. This rain forest is in Indonesia, in Southeast Asia.

South American rain forests are known for the brightly colored birds called macaws that live there.

forest are cut down each day. Some animals have lost so much of their habitat they have become endangered.

Many people now know how important the rain forest is. They are working hard to protect it. Let's learn more about some of the rain forest's endangered animals.

Rain Forest Climate

Do you know what climate is? It is the kind of weather a place has over time. Tropical rain forests tend to be warm and wet. Temperatures are around 80° F (27° C) most of the time. Temperate rain forests have cooler temperatures.

Orangutans are endangered apes that live in the rain forests of Indonesia and Malaysia.

In both kinds of rain forests, more than 55 inches (140 cm) of rain fall each year. Some tropical rain forests get as much as 400 inches (1,016 cm) of rainfall each year. That is a lot of rain!

Rain Forest Habitats

Rain forests are generally broken into four layers. The highest layer is the **emergent layer**. The tallest trees break through the **canopy** there. Eagles, bats, and monkeys can be found there. The upper canopy forms a leafy roof over the forest. Monkeys, insects, birds, and frogs live there.

Dusky leaf monkeys live in the canopy in rain forests in Southeast Asia.

The Madagascar day gecko is a lizard that lives in trees near the edge of rain forests.

The understory is below the canopy. It is made up of small trees, shrubs, and other plants. These plants must be able to grow with little sunlight. Jaguars, tree frogs, and insects live in this layer. The forest floor is the lowest layer. It is so dark that few plants grow there. Anteaters, insects, and snakes live in this layer.

The Rain Forest's Endangered Animals

Today more than 20 percent of the world's rain forests are gone. The animals on these pages are endangered mainly because people are taking over their homes to make cattle ranches, farms, mines, and logging businesses.

MAP KEY

■ Akepa
■ Tiger
■ Spider Monkey

■ Tree-Hole Crab
■ Sun Bear

Sun Bear

1. Sun Bear

Sun bears are listed as **vulnerable**. This means that their numbers are dropping quickly and they are likely to become endangered.

2. Akepa

There are about 14,000 akepas left in the rain forests of Hawaii. Habitat loss is one problem this bird faces.

Where Rain Forest Animals Live

Pacific Ocean
North America
Europe
Asia
Atlantic Ocean
Africa
South America
Indian Ocean
Australia
Southern Ocean
Antarctica

3. Tree-Hole Crab

This crab lives in water-filled tree holes. As people cut down rain forests, it makes it harder for this crab to find places to live.

Spider Monkey

4. Spider Monkey

Of the seven species of spider monkeys, two are **critically** endangered. The brown-throated spider monkey and the northern muriqui have lost 80 percent of their population.

5. Tiger

Three tiger **subspecies** have become **extinct** in the past 70 years. The six remaining subspecies are all endangered. The South China tiger has not been seen since the 1970s and may be extinct in the wild.

Tiger

Tigers are big cats that are in danger from **poachers** and habitat loss. It is thought that there are fewer than 2,500 tigers in the world.

Most Asian countries where tigers live have passed laws to keep these animals safe. They have put aside protected land as well. Even so, tiger

Some Bengal tigers have brown or black and white fur instead of orange, black, and white fur.

There are six subspecies, or kinds, of tigers. The tigers shown here are Bengal tigers, which live in rain forest habitats as well as grasslands and forests.

The Sumatran tiger is critically endangered. There are fewer than 300 of these tigers left.

numbers continue to fall. It is still worth trying to save tigers, though. In the 1940s, there were fewer than 40 Siberian, or Amur, tigers left in the Russian wild. Due to laws to stop poachers, Amur tigers' numbers have grown, although they are still endangered.

Spider Monkey

If you look up in the trees of a rain forest in Central America or South America, you might spot a spider monkey. Its long arms and **prehensile** tail let this monkey swing easily from branch to branch.

This female Geoffroy's spider monkey is carrying her baby on her back as she moves from branch to branch.

14

Spider monkeys' long prehensile tails are hairless at the end. This helps them grip tree branches.

Eight species of spider monkeys are endangered or critically endangered. These animals are in trouble due to hunting and habitat loss through **deforestation**.

The countries where spider monkeys live have put aside protected land, passed laws to limit hunting, and are working on **captive breeding** programs. Scientists hope these efforts will help spider monkeys make a comeback.

Puerto Rican Amazon

The Puerto Rican Amazon is a parrot that is native to the island of Puerto Rico. Its feathers are mostly green, with blue at the tips of its wings and red patches near its eyes. The parrot's coloring helps it blend in with its habitat in the rain forest canopy.

The Puerto Rican Amazon was once widespread but today is critically endangered.

The peregrine falcon is a bird of prey that lives all over the world. It is one of the Puerto Rican Amazon's predators.

People working to save this parrot have reintroduced the Puerto Rican Amazon into the wild.

The main threat it faces is habitat loss. People began efforts to save this bird from the edge of extinction in the 1960s. It is thought that only about 50 birds remain in the wild, although there are about 200 in captivity.

Sun Bear

The sun bear lives in tropical forests, including rain forests, in Southeast Asia. These **omnivores** eat termites, ants, beetle larvae, bee larvae, honey, fruits, and a few kinds of plants.

Scientists are not sure how many sun bears there are. They do know, though, that the number of bears has been falling. There has been a lot

Sun bears are vulnerable now, but they will become endangered if things do not change.

Sun bears have almost no natural predators. They can occasionally be overtaken and killed by tigers and reticulated pythons, like the one shown here, among other animals.

of deforestation in their habitat. People have been cutting down trees to make plantations or to harvest the trees for palm oil and other crops. In some places, fires caused by people have harmed forests where sun bears live. Another danger to sun bears is hunting.

Slow Loris

Slow lorises are a group of five species of **primates** that live in the rain forests of South Asia and Southeast Asia. They prefer to live high in the thick canopy. These large-eyed animals mostly hunt at night for bugs, eggs, fruits, and small animals.

Mountain hawk eagles are birds of prey that are slow loris predators.

The pygmy slow loris, shown here, is listed as vulnerable.

All five species are either vulnerable or endangered. One threat they face is deforestation, which causes habitat loss and leaves them with fewer places to live. They are also being taken from their habitat illegally and sold into the wildlife trade. People are working to enforce laws that protect these animals and their habitat.

Save the Rain Forest's Animals!

The rain forest is one of the most important **biomes** in the world. The Amazon rain forest alone is home to thousands of species of reptiles, birds, and mammals. It is also home to 30 million kinds of insects.

The tiny golden poison dart frog is an endangered animal that lives in Colombia's rain forests.

If people keep cutting down rain forests at the rate they are today, scientists think all rain forests could be gone in 40 years. That is why people are working hard to protect Earth's rain forests.

BIOMES (BY-ohmz) Kinds of places with certain weather patterns and kinds of plants.

CANOPY (KA-nuh-pee) The highest tree branches in a forest.

CAPTIVE BREEDING (KAP-tiv BREED-ing) Bringing animals together to have babies in a zoo or an aquarium instead of in the wild.

CRITICALLY (KRIH-tih-kuh-lee) Being at a turning point.

DEFORESTATION (dee-for-uh-STAY-shun) When most of the trees in a forest are cut down.

EMERGENT LAYER (ih-MER-jent LAY-er) The highest layer in a rain forest.

EXTINCT (ik-STINGKT) No longer existing.

OMNIVORES (OM-nih-vawrz) Animals that eat both plants and animals.

POACHERS (POH-cherz) People who illegally kill animals that are protected by the law.

PREHENSILE (pree-HEN-sul) Able to grab by wrapping around.

PRIMATES (PRY-mayts) The group of animals that are more advanced than others and includes monkeys, gorillas, and people.

SUBSPECIES (SUB-spee-sheez) Different kinds of the same animal.

VULNERABLE (VUL-neh-ruh-bel) Could be easily hurt.

Index

Websites

Due to the changing nature of Internet links, PowerKids Press has developed an online list of websites related to the subject of this book. This site is updated regularly. Please use this link to access the list: www.powerkidslinks.com/sea/rain/

24